A Real Messy Bitch

just along for the ride

christina bryers

BookLeaf Publishing

India | USA | UK

Made with ❤ on the BookLeaf Publishing Platform
www.bookleafpub.in
www.bookleafpub.com

Dedication

to every person i've collided with over the years
these are for you just as much as they're for me.

and for you, dad and ma.
always for you.

xoxo,
christina

Preface

life's a mess. isn't that preface enough?

Acknowledgements

special shoutout to sam and donny:
for letting me annoy you to death over my pieces and for
being the best hype mans.

and to my favorite lil man of all time: billy.
you're the best doggo and friend a girl could ask for.
(and if you could read, you'd kill me if you weren't in
here)

can you feel it still?

someone once told you that
there is a price to be paid
for every increase in consciousness.
you cannot be more sensitive to
p l e a s u r e
without being more sensitive to
p a i n

but your feelings are fluid
flowing like water down a creek
they melt into one another like hot lava
flooding your veins and your lungs
indistinguishable from one another
they crash into each other like tectonic plates
colliding violently behind your eyes
so intricately intertwined and convoluted
fusing together into muddled, perverted versions of
what they once were and from this –
only chaos can emerge

you feel everything
f e r v e n t l y,
        h e a v i l y,
  d e e p l y.

it's almost like the world is
too much for you.
but other people's feelings are
bland, tasteless,
shallow, simple.

and you are not simple.
you are complicated and intense and
fascinating and frustrating and passionate and
that is not something everyone knows how to love.
your mind and its beautiful way of
feeling pleasure, pain, and everything in between
all at once.
the way you can be so many different things
all at once.

perhaps it's merely side effects of that chaos
that dictates your every thought, emotion, behavior –
the chaos that rules you.

the same chaos that seeps into every part of your life.

tell us about the love you steered clear from last fall
and the friendship you let crumble away six months ago
and how you only seem to remember
when you touch things that are

colder than you.

can you feel it still?
the first time you dragged a blade across your wrist and
the first time you kissed the boy you loved and
how you couldn't tell the difference

it's not about you anymore

i saved myself
as well as i could.
so, maybe
nobody loves me.
maybe
nobody will ever love me.
but maybe
it's not about
being loved by someone else.
i tell myself that
someday this pain will be
useful.
maybe it will.
but then again,
maybe it won't.

i am so torn
between
being passionate
and
being psychological,
maybe i don't know
the difference.

scars

i've lost track of them all
each scar tells its own story –
stories, moments that i'll never recall.
i trace my fingers over the raised, pale worms
lined up and down my upper thighs.
i can't remember.
any of them.
how unbelievably pointless?

i can't remember why i felt the need to
create the ugliest kind of art
on my own skin and flesh –
constant reminders of all the days i felt
lost.
    alone.
        enraged.
            trapped in my own skin.

and there were so many of those days.

there are two i remember specifically.
i don't know why but the rest seemed to
fade away, and these two nuzzle their way
into the darkest corners of my mind.

the pale, permanent indent above my ankle.
i saw my bone and for the first time ever
i truly felt the impulsivity that results from
adolescence and mental illness colliding into each other.
every time i feel the deep divot from where the stitches
were,
i am reminded of how easily i could lose control.

a freckled over set of claw marks on my arm.
he was leaving and i was going to have to
take care of her all by myself.
i was only thirteen.
abandonment is all i feel whenever
i catch a glimpse of the scars, almost faded entirely
but never fully gone.

the blood dripping quickly in slow motion
down my arms or legs.
endorphins releasing and
the physical pain finally lets me feel something or
finally distracts me from the psychological pain.
that sense of control.
somehow these memories are comforting.

scars only tell where we've been and
they don't dictate where we're going

yet i look at my body, this body that i love,
littered with scars from wounds i inflicted on myself.
i feel disgusted. confused. ashamed.
how can i say i love myself
when i so clearly hate myself?

i've always said i choose to see them as battle scars,
as proof that i'd made it to the other side.

but have i?

homesick

i am homesick.
it's not something i thought i'd feel
after moving back home.
home.
where i grew up at least.

i can hear
the same harsh buzzing of cicadas in the wet, warm air.
the same ones that sang through the stickiness
every summer of my childhood.
ma and dad are both gone
and their absence lingers in the air.

a few months pass and
then comes the perpetual gloom of fall and winter;
incessant grey skies that keep me drowsy for months.
the same grey that plagued me for nearly twenty years.
the same grey that dampened my spirit
and wore down my strength year after year.
the same roads and corner stores
and parks and restaurants
remind me of the past.
the love, the laughter, the bliss of it all.
but the past also triggers

the trauma and anguish of a time forgotten –
the scars of wounds long healed over
ripping open all at once.
every familiar corner brings memories
pouring back or crashing into me.

is this home? because i am homesick.

i miss the warmth of the sunshine that melted
each day into night.
the familiar barstools that reached out to me,
reminding me of all the different souls i collided with
in such a short time.
i miss the comfort of going to my favorite spots:
one for coffee,
one for dessert,
one for breakfast sandwiches,
even one for cheese.
the first taste of each one on the tip of my tongue.

i almost wish i didn't know how
experiencing all four seasons can spoil a person.
and how the mountains bring you peace
merely with their presence.
i missed trekking through them,
feeling totally immersed.
i never thought i'd be able to love snow,

but this kind of snow wrapped you up
and kissed you on the forehead.
and man, those ugly tiled floors of the sandwich shop
where i found my chosen family
will always echo through my thoughts.
every familiar corner brings memories gushing back,
warmly embracing me.
is that what i'm homesick for?

i'm being yanked in two different directions,
nearly splitting myself in two.
just like that poor baby in the bible
that they were going to tear in half.
i'm homesick for a feeling.
i'm homesick for a family.
i'm homesick for a version of myself.
i'm homesick, but what is a home?
is it a place? is it the people in that place?
is it the hugs and the laughter and the tears?
the late nights and the smoke breaks and the kickbacks?
is it the hard times and the suffering and the pain?
is it where i healed? is it the people who healed me?

i don't know where home is anymore
but i am getting so very tired of feeling sick for home
and not knowing where the hell it is

this is me letting you go

this is me letting you go.

however it looks
however i feel
whatever i do

it is mine and mine alone
you are not a guest on the list

this is me letting you go.

and you're not invited to the party

the monster inside

i loved a boy once.
he used to kiss me like it was life or death,
like every kiss was our last.
he made me feel things that i'd forgotten i could feel.
when we touched, we melted into one another.

i felt like i was home.
he knew me, like really knew me.
he looked at me and didn't see what everyone else saw.
he would breathe me in,
see me in all my chaotic, messy glory
and he would still love me.
he loved me even more.

sometimes though
when i was taking a bubble bath
or smoking a joint
or just stuck in my head
i would think to myself:
he didn't know me – not truly.
he had yet to meet the darkness inside me,
the twistedness that took everything good
and made it into something ugly.
he had yet to find what was lurking underneath

all those tiny things he adored:
my eruptive laugh and that single dimple on my face and
how i sang way too loudly
in the shower, in the car, anywhere
and he didn't have the slightest inkling about
the void that festered within the woman
he was so in love with.

unknown to him, the woman he fell in love with
wasn't here anymore.
it held me in its clutches;
it had grown into more than just a part of me
it had become so tangled with the very core of my being
that sometimes
i couldn't tell what was me anymore.
or was it all me?
it had begun feeding on my soul,
devouring chunks of me little by little.
feeling more and more hollow,
i forced my soul into the deepest, darkest corner of
myself i could find.
i had to stop it before it destroyed me completely,
leaving my body an empty shell ruled by something that
only lives to feed off those i love.

a constant battle was raging inside of me,
and i could only suppress my hunger for

his love and his time and his touch for so long.
the monster was breaking through
and i couldn't hold it back for much longer.
one bite with its razor-sharp teeth and
all that love and life
would be drained right out of him
feeding the monster and starving my soul.
or was it the other way around?

i didn't want to take anything away from him.
i loved everything about him but now when we were together,
i felt like merely a passenger in my own body.
i was paralyzed, trapped inside myself
watching the love we shared evaporate
as loving me wore him down.

he entertained this idea of love with someone
who had become a stranger for as long as he could
without losing himself entirely.
he convinced himself to stay
he thought he could still see me sometimes,
in glimpses.
only a flicker here and there
but that was enough for him,
until it wasn't.

until he couldn't see me at all anymore.
the monster that had taken so much from me
just kept taking and taking and taking.
my relationships deteriorated and
the connection to my soul felt weaker;
so weak that sometimes i couldn't feel it at all.
i worried that it may have withered
and died in some dark corner;
turned to dust, never to be found again.

i couldn't blame him for leaving me.
how could he maintain a relationship with someone
so excessively alive one moment and
so excessively dead the next?
that would start to eat away at him.
he wanted to save me, fix me, fuck me but
he couldn't have extracted my soul
from all the places it was hiding,
and even if he could,
he wouldn't have known how to love
what he discovered.
and that's okay.
we were what we were when we needed it.

perhaps the monster and i have been the same all along.
perhaps that boy and i
grew into something we never saw coming.

perhaps the monster was never a monster at all.
perhaps the reality of me:
beautiful and terrifying and strange
was too much for that boy.
perhaps i am not made of things
everyone knows how to love.

to the next boy to love me:
crawl inside this body of mine,
find me where i am hollow, dark, tangled.
be able to love me there, too.

it feels like shit

"so how does it feel?"

"how does what feel?"

"to be perfect, absolutely perfect in every way?"

"it feels like shit."

do not call me perfect.
a lie isn't a compliment.
call me an erratic
unhinged, damaged
and insecure mess.

then tell me that you
love me for it.

anxiety

you don't understand why i can't breathe,
why i'm shaking and screaming and clawing at my face.

i have a friend.
one that defies the loneliness that engulfs me.

when i'm sobbing to the stars
and screaming at the moon,
the sky is not all that i have.
when my chest feels like it's been ripped open
and my head may explode,
i know my body is a house
still very much intact.

she lets me come and go as i need
like the shore lets the sea.
a vulnerability so scary but so great.

she is beautiful,
but she has been sad
and i am grateful that she understands.

i have a lover.
one that tastes like everything i've ever adored.

i look at him with something more
agonizing than love and more
exhilarating than lust.
an ache deeper than my bones
and too violent for my veins.

when i am trapped inside myself,
i feel his lips
burning holes in my skin.

he is everything
and i know that is wrong
but i don't care.

i have a friend,
one that looks at the boy i love
and loses her breath.

i have a lover.
one who tries to reason with me
when i worry so much that i cry.

but she is fumbling with the buttons on his shirt and
he is taking off her skirt with his teeth.
i wonder what his name tastes like
when she sighs it into his mouth

and what i would find if i followed the trail
of scars his lips left behind on her skin.
she is tracing his muscles with her fingers and
his hands are crawling between her thighs.
she can feel the wet heat of his breath and
see the ring of yellow around his pupils,
and he thinks –
this is home.

i am not lingering in the air.
i am not running through their veins.

so please –
tell me how to breathe.

my mother and i

my mother didn't deserve
what she went through
but neither did i.

i remember consoling her
as she sobbed and
praying to whatever god i could muster up
that she would be happy
eventually, finally

she was beauty and depression
and chaos and love
and laughter and terror.
she could be so bright but
when that light became dark,
she chose to wander in it
let it overtake her
until she was lost
without any hope of a way back

in so many ways i am my mother.
and i loved my mother fiercely
but i don't want to be like my mother -
i want to be happy before i die

my mother didn't deserve
what she went through
but neither did i.

nothing

it's hard to feel you like this
when all i can remember is
the long nights the sex so raw and real
the hours spent stoned on your couch
the way my hand fit entirely in yours
the way we never had to talk but
never ran out of things to say to each other
the way we were never tired of each other
every day wasn't enough we needed more
now i don't know what you like about me
i think nothing.

drunk

i'm drunk.
where are you?

how is it
       my dear
that you make me feel   like this?

i hate everything
               but you.

you are my umbrella
but even so
you are the rain,   you bastard.

why do you have to look at
me   like that?

sighing it, tasting it
but forbidding myself to let it slip

              not even a whisper.

it's agonizing

                    vehement
  insistent, h e a v y

but you are not here.
where are you?

it's jumping o

                    u

                         t the window,
shattering the mirror,
throwing itself across the room.

crawling in between my legs

                                   my fingers

                                                    my

lips

where you should be.

i'm swimming in it
it's flooding my veins
                         sinking
sunk.

but i can't say it,   why
can't i say it?

let them starve

i am reading an article about elephants.
something that couldn't possibly remind me of you.

did you know that elephants are
one of the only mammals capable of
experiencing emotions and empathy.
and they're one of less than ten animals
that can recognize themselves in a mirror.

they are emotionally intelligent
and their emotional experiences are
close resemblances to those of humans.

they can recognize and respond
to the pain and sadness
felt by other elephants in their herd
by emitting a low-frequency sound
when distressed that signals their herd
to soothe them by stroking their trunk.

elephants even mourn their dead like humans do –
ritualistically honoring and respecting
the bodies and bones of their dead
before the inevitable time comes to say

goodbye or may we meet again or i love you

elephants can actually die of heartbreak.
when their mate dies, the elephant left behind
sobs wildly before collapsing entirely,
either refusing to or unable to get up.
other elephants try to comfort them but
the elephant remains frozen in place on the ground –
literally starving themselves until they die.

i catch myself wiping a tear,
your absence having a familiarity i despise.
i wish that i could tell you that
my feelings for you are exactly like those elephants.
i can't take something that big, that powerful –
and snap my fingers, make them disappear.

i can't shoot them.
i can't poison them.
i can't see any other way except

let them starve.

we never made it, did we?

i know what we are --
and i know what we aren't.

it's like you were red and
i was blue but once you touched me
i was a hue of violet and
you said purple just
wasn't for you

and i've got too much soul
to be loved by someone
who has never known passion.

they say the sea speaks more honestly
to those willing to drown --
i dunk my head under without thought
and you barely dip your toes in at the shore.

i could use you to fill
the emptiness echoing inside me.
but i don't want to because
i think i did love you at one point and
nothing really goes away for good,
it's always here. always

then suddenly, i felt nothing.

29

we never made it, did we?

thieves

like thieves, we are all in love with stolen hearts.

i fell for you the way we fall asleep:
slowly, then all at once.

and i tend to love people who
don't love me back.

so i think i'm starting to love you
but i don't know what to do
because it's taking over,
completely washing over me.
overwhelming me.
but you're just out of grasp.

i want you any way i can get you,
and not only because you're cute and clever
and sexy and kind and you laugh at all my jokes --
although god knows you are all of those things --
but because i don't think i want to wake up
and live another day without you in it.

but your heart is spoken for.
you say she's boring and controlling

you say you aren't in love with her,
even after all this time.
but it's the comfortable decision
so you stay.

but let me ask you this:
does she make your heart beat faster than i do?
and when you breathe her name and mine
in the same breath,
do they taste the same?

many people will love the idea of you
but will lack the maturity to handle
the reality of you, so tell me:
does she ever make you miss yourself?

it's okay to forgive yourself
for loving the wrong person.

i have to forgive myself
for loving the wrong person.
all the time.

i didn't see this coming.
friend vs lover
what a selfish debate.

so instead i'll drink until i'm happy
and smoke until i can't think
and i'll fish for compliments
from those i don't want them from
and i'll wonder what you're doing
and what you're feeling
and who you're with
but i won't call.

like thieves, we are all in love with stolen hearts.

sometimes

sometimes i get sad when i think about you,
because i'm not sure if you'll miss me when i'm gone.

because when i look at you i see that sparkle in your
eyes,
                but you aren't looking at me.

because when i grab your hand or kiss your cheek,
             you don't giggle or even smile.

because when you do smile,
i don't know why
             and you don't tell me.

sometimes i get sad when i think about you
because you avoid meeting my eyes
and even when you don't
             i see nothing in yours.

because you're somewhere else.
looking at someone else's face
hearing someone else's words
            but i don't know where you are.

sometimes i get sad when i think about you
because you tell me everything's fine
                    and deny your distance.

but i see you fighting that smirk.

sometimes i get sad when i think about you
because you tell me you can't talk
              and you don't have time for this

and you scream when i beg you to stay on the phone.

because you aren't saying anything
because you aren't trying to calm me down
because i hear it draining out of you

sometimes i get sad when i think about you
because you want to care
                          but you don't

because you feel nothing
 but exhaustion when you look at me

because those words always echo in my head.

sometimes i get sad when i think about you
because i know you're with him.
    because i know that's where you've always been.

sometimes i get sad when i think about you
because i know if i call,

        you won't answer

because you didn't cry or scream
      or feel anything at all

because i knew you were never going to miss me.

sometimes i get sad when i think about you
because i see the way you look at him,

and because you never once looked at me like that.

how dare you want more?
part i

yes,
i want more
how could i not?
my feelings for you aren't small.
they're all encompassing.

yet i am barely a fraction of your life
barely a fleeting thought through your brain.

when we're together,
i feel the sparks between us starting fires
embers falling slowly around us
but the blaze burns me until
i remember the reality that i will
inevitably slither back to:
familiar, lonely, cold.
the place that smothers any fire left
in me, for you. it chokes it out of me
before i'm entangled in your perfidious grasp.

that one that reminds me, i don't know you.
i want to but i can't
because you won't let me.

you'll dodge my questions and
brush me off and act like
i am unreasonable for wondering at all and
i am crazy for finding your reluctance suspicious.

the empty beer cans and
glasses littering your tables
the ruffled sheets and the two bowls
left at the table.
the remnants of the part of you i don't know,
that you don't let me know,
that maybe i am scared to know.

why won't you let me know you?
and even if you did, would it be you that i knew?

i grasp at every opportunity to feel important
to you: significant, irreplaceable, missable
like a beautiful oak tree that stands for generations
and is noticed the second it is hacked down.

but i don't know that i ever will be.
so why can't i let you go?

how dare you want more?
part ii

i think of
kissing you holding you laughing with you

do you even think of me?
i know you don't –
you only ever think of yourself.

i want more than once a week
and late nights
and last minute plans.
your couch and your car
and your bed and your balcony.

i want to be all you can think about
i want you to not be able to
sleep or eat or breath without me.

but instead, you are indifferent.
i am merely a commodity in your life.
yet i think i'm in love with you
and i hate myself for it.

because i'm not in love

not with you, nor anyone else
yearning to be wanted, to be loved.
i grasp at the possibility of something
real and raw and full of passion
just like i grasp at your attention and
grasp at those big feelings i have for you.
except they aren't real.
you aren't real.

i tell myself it should be over.
it's over it's over it's over –
please be over.
i cannot be reeled in by your deceit again
or i may shatter into a million pieces
unsure how to put myself back together.

so i am back in the four walls of my bedroom
looking at the same nikon camera and the same
polaroids of memories filled with laughter and love and
passion – something you've never felt
for anything at all.
the same books surround me and
the same candles crackle around me.
i am here.
you are not.

you are not.

but were you ever?

this year

this year
i met the most broken version of myself
but also the strongest.

this year
i had my heart shattered
by friends and men alike.
but then it healed with
a little help from my friends

this year
i grieved both my parents
for the second time
and it was sad and nostalgic
and a little bit easier
than last year.

this year
i was broke and stressed,
unstable and burned out.
i went from job to job
until one showed me
growth i'd never known.
it showed me people

i didn't think i'd find.

this year
i worked on myself
as i have for the last 14 years
but this year was different.
i looked deeper
at all the ugly and wonderful
faced my truth, accepted my circumstances,
cut people off, let people go
then celebrated the person
that came out on the other side.

this year
i met the most broken version of myself
but also the strongest.

a beautiful life

you can still build a beautiful life
for yourself
even if you lost years of it
to grief
to mental illness
to a wound that won't heal
to addiction
to someone that hurt you
to darkness

but you need to believe that.
please believe that
you can build a beautiful life for yourself

head first

and again,

i dive in head first
knowing that
all that awaits me
is one big. fucking. mess.

the dumb shit we do
for even the slightest chance
at love.

leaving

you leave and
i start feeling the way you do after sex,
when one person finally gets out of bed
and you lie there pulling the sheets up.
that unheld feeling –
a blind blurriness.
not neediness but a sort of twistedness –
an absence that echoes through you.

the way you tug at your naked earlobe
when you lose an earring.
the way you run your fingers over a scar
after the wound has healed.

you leave,
and i start thinking of ways to leave me too.